Jacob Polley

Jackself

PICADOR

First published 2016 by Picador
an imprint of Pan Macmillan,
20 New Wharf Road, London N1 9RR
Associated companies throughout the world
www.panmacmillan.com

ISBN 978-1-4472-9044-5

A CIP catalogue record for this book is available from the British Library.

Printed and bound by CPI Group (UK) Ltd, Croydon, CR0 4YY

This book is dedicated

to my mum

and

to my dad

ACKNOWLEDGEMENTS

I'd like to thank *Bare Fiction Magazine, Ploughshares, Poetry* (Chicago), *The Poetry Review* and *The Verb* on BBC Radio 3 where versions of a few of these poems first appeared. Thanks to John Alder, for his magnificent and provocative setting of the poems. *Jackself* had the privilege and benefit of two early readers, Jean Sprackland and Katharine Towers, who gave me great encouragement and to whom I am most grateful.

Contents

Soul, self; come, poor Jackself . . .
G.M. Hopkins

By a knight of ghosts and shadows
I summoned am to tourney
  Ten leagues beyond
  The wide world's end
Methinks it is no journey
Anon.

The House that Jack Built

the first trees were felled
and sailed in, wrecked, then slept
an age in the northern sun, blackening
to iron   were found by horsemen
leading their horses and raised as
cloud's axles, rafters of night, a god's gates
     were passed through, seen
from miles off, rolled the sun
and moon along their lintels, rooted,
put out leaves   for a second time
creaked, tasted the rain, held
the wind to their hearts while
the horsemen streamed like
their horses' manes
into the dark, their fires
black smudge in the subsoil, their bridles
of gold underground

     lived long, grew great
                    were a second time
felled, dressed   were sharpened to stakes
and raised as a fort
by farmers who'd followed their ploughs
to the treeline for fuel
to bake the pots
their ashes were buried in
with a scattering of grain

like stars   each small clay
heaven still hangs in the earth

   were overgrown,
steered clear of
   called dragon's ribs
         devil's cot   were nested among, rotted
down beside
   harboured foxglove, eggshell,
owl pellet, primrose, honeycomb
   were glazed, split,
put out buds of malachite, blossoms
of salt, grew again, put out
small translucent fruits named
by the women who prized them
teardrops, ice apples, clarities
   were offered bread,
dolls of woven grass, plaits of hair, coins
with the obverse ground smooth, beads
of turquoise

   twisted, straightened, filled
with rooks, held again
the wind to their hearts, creaked, scraped
off the sunlight's scales with their leaves, were
a grove, grew
manes of lichen, were murmured
under, gave counsel on still nights
of open doorways the dead came through
on horseback or shouldering flails or bearing chimes

of ice apples   gave shelter
    were felled for it, their roots
ripped up by a legion's engineers
and left like brainstems
rucked on the earth

    were timber but the pitsaws
snarled in their rings of iron
    broke teeth on the flints
that welted their sapwood
    were good
for nothing, stacked, fired, marched
away from, sucked up the flames,
hissed, smoked, glowed blood-
black, were tempered, twice-
forged   bided
on site as battle-stain,
in story as Head Wood

    lay half-buried, grown over, still hot
                were stumbled upon
by navigators, hit
with hammers and rang
until they were made lock gates
to slam
shut on the slow wet
    grew green, slime-
faced, knew runoff, weird particulates,
held fast against drizzle's
tonnage, the nudge

[3]

and bonk of a bloater   were left
stinking when the water died

    stood strange in currents
of deep grass, open wide
    flexed, hungered once more
for the light, bulged, branched, rived
out of their lacquer, unfurled
leaves of oilskin, shook down clots
of blossom   lived
long, grew great
    weren't felled but walled in, roofed
over, giving span
to a farmhouse, hanging
a hall from their outstretch, bracing floor
after floor on their inosculating
joists, which sang
to a barefoot tread and were called
home of shadows   heart of the wind
    Lamanby

Every Creeping Thing

By leech, by water mite
by the snail on its slick of light
    by the mercury wires
    of the spiders' lyres
and the great sound-hole of the night

By the wet socket of a levered stone
by a dog-licked ice cream cone
    by spores, mildew
    by the green *atchoo*
by the yellow split pea and the bacon bone

All the doors must have their way
and every break of day its day
    instead of a soul
    Jackself has a coal
and the High Fireman to pay

By head-lice powder, Paraquat
snapdragon's snap and rat-tat-tat
    who's at the door
    of the door of the door
it's Jackself in his toadskin hat

Jack Sprat

who depends
on strong drink and soft food   gives Jackshit
   comprehends
fearlessly by mouth, lacquering bricks and bottles with curatorial spit

  who watches Thomascat
stalk the sliding light across the hearthrug on afternoons
of his limited Jackspan, none of which he can get back
   not the suns and moons
of it, not the crackling fur, lavender and turpentine smell of it

  who mumbles his greens, his fists, the bars
of his cage   whose one-piece suit isn't nightmare-
retardant   who is driven round and round in strangers' cars
for comfort   who can achieve unawares,
like Thomascat, aloof   only to be turned upon by those minted ladies
he'd brought so low before him

  whose face is reset hourly
     whose mind is solid fear
      whose trades are none and all
the possible   who will come into anthracite,
corbel, gasometer, throstle
  who gnaws boot- and book-leather alike
     who covets the onion
wrapped in plain brown onion skin
  whose small memory is a gift that makes
the world over again
when he wakes

The Goodies

goody on you goody sweet
smell goody goody touch
   goody butter, goody meat
goody shoes on goody feet
   a goody cake with six
goody candles to yank
the goody shadows round
by their goody hair

   goody blow goody out
goody fire's little spikes
   breathe goody in
then pop the goody squeak-face with a goody silver pin

   no wishing it wouldn't be
or wasn't or would better be
   no wondering how so hard it hurts,
just two goody thumbs and a goody peephole
for goody staring, goody weepers, standing goody by
in nothing but your goody suit with goody in your eye

   goody easy goody true
        who's the goody   goody you!
              goody up the goody staircase with a goody creak
to watch the moving pictures on the screen of goody sleep

no worrying the world to shreds
no going blind or blue
just a choice of face on waking from a dozen goody heads

thank goody goody dust do goody do
or you'll be trapped with one grey face your baddy pokes right through

Jackself's Quality

can't be bought
or stolen   Mudder hasn't bottled it
   Mugginshere hasn't brought it home
in his briefcase
   the farmer hasn't clipped its weighty foam
from his blackest sheep
   the hawk-man, with a rag of meat
in his leather glove, can't bring it
stooping from the sky   Thomascat
hasn't fetched it from the farmyard
to lay still warm at Jackself's feet

   the dark continent
Jackself peels from the flank
of a Friesian cow, ties to his ankles
and drags across the flatland
at midday, doesn't prove
his substance   the night
is made of what he needs

   he moonwalks in daylight,
afraid like snow he'll wane or drift
before he can hold
the road out front, the fields behind
and the earth in the churchyard
   so Jackself crawls to the coal-shed
and eats

The Lofts

Jackself has climbed into the lovely lofts
of Lamanby, their floors ankle-deep
in silver dust and the floorboards
spongy with woodworm

    in the attic corners great cauls
of cobweb hang from crusty chains, frayed rope, horse tack
and the skeletons of past Selves, their skulls
packed with sea salt and tea-leaves   Edwardself, Billself
    Wulfself with scraps of his shaggy self still attached
            alas   in the vaulted gloom
sunbeams fizz
off a canine here and there
a gold medallion
that flares from its nest
of spider-grey chest-hair

    back they go, the Selves
        Aself, Oxself and coracle-ribbed, ape-armed Selfself,
his ochred bones trophied in a flaky niche in the clay wall

Jackself holds his pullovered forearm
to Selfself's flute-like radius, which swivels
in the draught   soon,
Jackself murmurs, and every Self skeleton
clinks   thanks a fucking bunch, Jackself cries
and his cry echoes back
echoes back   the mouse in the hope chest
nibbling the cuff
of Annself's unworn wedding gown
stiffens its whiskers   the ghost of Billself's army pony flicks an ear
and paws
the unshiftable dust and Selfself sings a silent song of the horned whale
and the white bear

        Jackself, if only you'd found that meteorite
at the bottom of the coal hod
or that necklace of eagle claws
strung from the handle of the skylight
        but you were too afraid to stay and hear
the silence that was yours
by birth, and back you thundered down the stairs

Lessons

the names of things and their relations, adding and taking away
    Jackself is taken away
from the rest of the class and added
to a corner most days
    days that stink of cow-gum,
mouldy silence and the screech
of Miss Clout's chalk stick on the blackboard

    a wall is for staring at
    a desk for sleeping at
    Jackself can do that

    there's nothing to read and the world's written
backwards   at lunchtime Mr Workbench, the Headmaster,
moans the Lord's Prayer and everyone
and Jackself must join in

    Jackself has many trespasses
but no daily bread
is baked in the school's ovens
    he must ask the dinner-ladies' forgiveness
for the cartilage stew and spreadable carrots
the flavour of warm steel tins

    a floorboard's for eating off
    a fart for letting off
    get thee, Jackself, to the trough

for you are pig-slow, a starey calf
and can't even hold a pencil stub
in your hooves to letter   *see,*
Miss Clout says to Mugginshere,
see what he's written all these hours and days
    and she shakes the sugar-paper sheet
of wobbly noughts

    standing over her, Mr Workbench solemnly inclines
his one-thought-
at-a-time head
    but Jackself's far

and away
    his mind a corner
of beehives
    his fingers a box of matches
        his nose the afternoon rain
            his ears yesterday
                his eyes green eyes
                    his tongue an earwig
before it hatches

Applejack

by hedgehog path
and badger path, Jackself
happens with the clouds
into sunlight   water-
damaged sky, silver in the floor
and Jackself on all fours,
his skin skin his
talk all gone
    hound's tongue oxeyes
birdsfoot rosehips
    grain of the wind
in a buzzard's wing
bones, empty as the sky
    crab apples oak apples applejack
        cold
under his ink cap,
holes in his foxgloves, his
foot leather black
and supple now he knows
his own mind with it   goes
by cattle grid
and cattle trough, icy
sloshings in him   fears
the dog
and Lucy Fur, who
glints at night
where he trembles, shut in

everywhere with his own
heartrush and the trees' roar
   a white root
threading the muck
under a rotted log
wakes him
   bent pale stalks,
leaves let go
to dry-curl and turn on the surface
of the sky, small
panes of it where the
tarmac gives out
   he returns
nowhere to somewhere by
standing there
in sunlight, its flicking
over him like   likelike
   he's been this way
before he couldn't
remember any way but
onwards and upwind
   along a fence-line
to see what's hanging, down
in a ditch where the still
dark stands

Peewit

a little one
    drab   barely skyborne, with nothing
of the gut-unravelling acumen
of the scavenger   this is Jackself
limping across marshland, making a decoy
of himself, piping up when the day goes dim
so close to the ground he's almost it

    small wonder Peewit
is the name the other boys have given him
    not Jackdaw, not Rook

      the gods of bracken and fly-tipped
black plastic sacks will expose themselves to the pilgrim
who has faith in the star
at the centre of the crab apple, in the ditchful
of frogspawn and the shed door
hinged with spiders' webs

    so it comes to pass
for Peewit, whippy stick in his right hand

as he tramps the far-out lanes with those
who had diminished him,
a breeze
starts to ratch in the dust   the foxglove
jangles   his legs
break and he goes down, his eyes a white
flutter in his head

    the boys circle him
where he fits,
grinding his teeth so hard they sing
    and when they heft him,
heavier than he should be,
his bird-soul batters
into him   they process so slowly the light's
all gone by halfway home
    when

Peewit's no longer between them   has flown
    and blank with terror
the boys go round and round
in the dark and cold and are not ever found

The Goose Shed

Jackself finds Jeremy Wren
in the goose shed   who the fuck
has a goose shed, Wren says

 people with geese,
Jackself says   he's standing in the bright
door square, his shadow-self
monstered against the dim back wall
where Wren crouches, stringy knees
drawn up to his chin
  where are they then, Wren says

    Jackself looks at his shoes
     they prefer not to use
the goose shed, he says

 it's true the goose and gander hiss
and thrash with blazing wings
anyone who dares set foot
on Lamanby's yard,
but they nest in among
the elder brush behind the barn

while the ghost shed
is where Jackself comes to hunker down
in the gold straw
and watch Lamanby's sandstone doorstep

and red front door,
as if from outside his own life and not
minding as it goes on without him

    you mean
the goose shed, Wren says   everybody's got
a ghost shed

    have they, Jackself says, taken aback
       yeah,
course, Wren says   somewhere
to take yourself off to, just close enough
to hear your mum,
dad, brother and sister
laughing
but not to make out
what they're laughing at   it wouldn't be right,
he says, to overhear

    no, Jackself says,
but what are you doing in my shed
    I'm looking for ghost eggs, Wren says,
and you're standing in my light

Nightlines

Jackself and Jeremy Wren are setting
nightlines in the kidney-coloured pool
all the streams of England run into
    Jackself's fretting

    all night the guiled
will hang, their hooked lips
mouthing into the waterworks and bloodstreams
of all England

    all night, gaffed,
their bullion flexing
until Jeremy Wren
bashes them at dawn with his hardwood priest

    Wren,
who says his granddad built the southern domes
Jesus needed to stable His beasts,
thinks Jackself's a soft-lad, a quick-
tear, a worry-wit,
and ties off another triple-barbed spinner

so Jackself rolls up his jeans,
takes one end of the nylon line looped to a tent peg and
wades into the chuckling shallows   slippery-stoned ice-cool
fishpath where no one has stood

for a thousand years   when Wren's not looking
Jackself stamps his foot
and all the carp and sticklebacks, the perch and pike and bream
are shaken out
of their gullible, muddy-minded dream

Cheapjack

as an elephant has memory
so Jeremy Wren has merchandise
    in his pocket, an order book,
a Biro behind his ear, and in his palm
a matchbox from which he offers
Jackself *the patter*, eight-legged
and shrivelled like a dead
star

    wrap your tongue round this,
he says, and sell a man
a second shadow

    isn't it an old spider,
Jackself says   you have to learn to overlook
your own eyes,
Wren says, otherwise
you'll never live the life you might
    he slides shut the little drawer
and stows the matchbox back in his jacket

    that night
Jackself lies awake,
his commercial inhibitions coming undone
in the dark and hiss of the rain

and next day at school he's barking the corridor
in a sandwich board that proclaims
    a belt of Eden serpent's skin
    a fairy's skull, a stone age stone
    a map of sleep, a stick of rock
    from Pompeii's only sweetie shop
    a pick n mix of famous stains
    a hanged man's jerk, a traffic cone
    a bedbug from the riverbed
    an ominous pencil, a furry mint
    the last gold hair from Satan's head

The Whispering Garden

listen to those hollyhocks
   those lupins,
Wren says   I've watched the bees
stealing in and out
with their furry microphones
to record the voices inside

   I've put my ear to the box
where they take the noise
only to be warned
that an eye
was on me
all the time   look!
he says, scrambling to his feet

   in the crook
of Jackself's elbow
a Wall Brown butterfly
blinking its wings

It

tell us what's wrong, Jeremy Wren,
crouched in the corner, spitting no blood,
robust in bladder and bowel, your toes
untouched by fire or flood
    no cold wind blows
        there's hair on your feet and mint
in your groin and tonight
is milk, tomorrow cream
and the day after that
a herd that lows
from your very own
meadowland of light

    your head doesn't hurt
though it's bigger inside
than out   Jeremy Wren,
whole of heart,
tell us what pains you

    my hole is bigger inside than out
and the heart of my pain
is a black bull's heart
and the tongue of my pain
a black bull's tongue that every day
licks off the cream
of the light   there's hair in my bowel and doubt
in my groin and my head's full of
animal glue

I'm spending my face
on people of fire
who visit at night
to stare at my emptiest place
while I crouch in the corner
and read my own spit
with a torch for a clue
    that's it

Les Symbolistes

way out among the hedgerows, Jackself
and Jeremy Wren, drunk
on white cider and Malibu,
are kicking up dust, the froth
of the cow-parsley spunk
or cuffs of sweat-yellowed cambric,
the seamy side ablaze in the moonlight
and fancy words on Jackself's tongue
now the locks of his head are picked
and the distance he's kept from his different selves
is all undone

    how good it feels to be French
and deranged, swinging the empty crock
of his desire

    what the fuck,
Wren says   my dad sniffed fag-
smoke on my breath and made me eat
a twenty pack, then welted me
buckle-first
when I asked what was for sweet

fie, foh and fum
    I smell your backwash in the coconut rum

      Jackself giggles and tilts the bottle nightwards   starburst
and the spinning moon's bone china rim

my dad sniffed himself
on me, Jackself says, and made me eat him
carved so thin
I could read a rose-tinted poem through each slice

    A POEM! Wren roars
      you're creepy as a two-headed calf
and I've always thought so

    but Jackself's bent double
in the dark, clutching his thighs,
a silver thread unspooling from his chin
    around him maze the midnight lonnings
of reasonable England
    see, Wren says, clapping Jackself on the back
as he retches   that's a proper poem for you
    agony to bring up,
with real carrots in it

An Age

Jackself is staying in
today, like a tool in a toolbox,
to try to *just be*
    high in the lovely lofts
of Lamanby
he stands at a cracked
window watching the gulls
flash and snap, like washing on a line

    in the pale heat
the wormy heartwood floorboards
swell and creak

    he stands for an age
        not for a dark age,
not for an ice age or an iron age, but for a
pollen age, when bees
browsed the workshops
of wildflowers for powder
of light, and the cables
of a spider's web were dusted with gold
by the unreceptacled breeze

Jack Frost

Jackself is tapping
fractals of ice, ice
ferns and berries of ice,
onto windowpanes and door handles, doorsteps,
grass blades and the postbox as he walks
the November village after midnight

    he's wearing his homemade thousand-milk-bottle-top
winter suit,
complete with epaulettes
of copper wire, and the lametta wig
he's kept all year in the Auto-Arctic Unit
that hums in the cellar beneath Lamanby

    but it's hard going, all this tapping every boot-scraper
and hubcap, and 3 a.m. finds Jackself
with his silvery head
in his hands, slumped on the unspun roundabout
among the gallows-poles of the moonlit playground,
the stars grinding on above him
    his suit tinkles as he shivers

would it really all go to shit
if he went home before sunrise, leaving untouched a gutter-trickle
here or a windscreen there
    fuck it
                Jackself wants a hot chocolate and a digestive biscuit
                    he wants his bed
and doesn't need to be doing this
cold scrollwork,
this archiving
of air bubbles
and tatty leaves

    he hauls himself to his feet, gives
the roundabout a heave
and crunches across the grass   but who's this weaving down the empty road
wearing snow-globe deely boppers, a mantle of tinsel and gauntlets and greaves
of kitchen foil

    it's Jeremy Wren,
waving a glitter-sprinkled wooden spoon
at the wing-mirrors of parked cars and the street lamp's
long case, baking them in frost
    you look a proper sight, Jackself says
                Wren's weeping the lucid mask that's welding to his cheekbones
                    help me, he says, keep everything just as it is

Plantation

Jackself's chinning
into the near-dark north wind
and feels it drawing silver thorns
from the corners of his eyes   he hunches
deeper into his parka,
deeper into his lion's mane
hood   I'm in the wilderness   no, he says,
I am the wilderness, where stray
greyhounds, scrawny prophets
and secret-keepers walk cold acres
hunting shelter under a welder's
mask moon, motherless
and fatherless, with no cupboard of sweetcorn
and baked-bean tins, no airtight
canisters of shortbread
          no baubles, no toilet paper, no featherbed

          what would a turned-out
greyhound want with baubles and toilet paper

          concave and zithery, they're the hounds
Jackself knows from the kennels down the lane
and, knowing no prophets,
he imagines a greyhound-ish
greybeard up on his withered hind legs
and leaning on a chewed dog-stick
to howl like the wind that's threshing these
trees, grown too fearsome to be Christmas trees

Blackjack

it's rained for days and Jackself
is standing under Lamanby's dripping eaves
to ask all
his dark questions in one go

    where does the toilet water take
his tapped-out gold, how many eggs
are laid by spiders at night in his nose
and did the bathwater once carry
his mucky portrait   (a skin on the water's surface, like engine oil)
down

down into galleries
of fungal brick, where a frog-faced haaf-
netter stood, midstream, to haul
the likeness of Jackself's naked body
from the current on an old bedsheet
and pin it up with the thousand others,
contorted on the sewer walls

    Jackself shudders   to be known secretly,
intimately   to be chronicled   get a grip
    who'd be interested in where I stand or what
I eat
or if my bathwater tastes, as it does, of lime cordial
and the future, which came as a shock
when I first began to
drink it instead of pulling the plug

the rain's turning to sleet
          snakes eat their old skins,
dogs their own sick
     Jackself steps out from under the eaves and squats
to give his reflection in the first puddle
on the gravel path
a lick

Snow Dad

won't he do,
Jackself says, longing at the red
front door of Lamanby
    behind the door is the great hall
and black stove he and Jeremy Wren could be
sitting in front of
with buttered crumpets and sugary tea,
taking turns to gob on the hotplate and consider
each frothy gob's
bead-dance and shrivel to a brief darkness
on the iron

    WAKE UP
Wren yells, and Jackself starts
back into snow-glare and the cold
that's radiating from the white
nine-foot dad Wren's
had them build to replace his own

    if you go to sleep, that'll be it,
Wren says   I climbed
into a chest freezer once
and before I could tell my lolly from my lick-stick
I was tucked up toasty warm,
a bag of petit pois for a pillow   there's no dreaming,
he says, when you're dead

what do you want a new old
man for anyhow, Jackself says, shivering

so I can give him a smile
stonier than a lip smile
    poke myself
in the eyes on his hand sticks
    run clean through him
and leave a me-hole
    hide a penny in his body
so when he's gone, I get it back

Pact

Jeremy Wren puts a finger-pistol
to his temple
and fires

    Jackself steps off
a thirteenth floor

    hold on, hold on,
Wren says

    you can't speak, Jackself says,
your head's blown off

    if I can't, you can't,
Wren says

    I'm still falling, Jackself says,
his arms rigid
at his sides

    quick then,
write a note, Wren says   and write one for me
while you're at it

    I can't write you a note,
I don't know why you've done it

I'll tell you, Wren says, just get your pen
and pocketbook out of your pocket
and scribble yours
before you hit the ground

   Jackself sighs
but does as he's told
     what have you written, Wren says

      I'm not telling you

               what,
Wren says, and narrows his eyes
    you think I don't have my own reasons
           I'll show you, he says,
and he storms home, stamps upstairs,
throws a dressing-gown cord
over the rafter in his bedroom,
pulls the slipknot over his head
then kicks away the women's underwear
catalogues he's balancing on
and hangs thinking fuck I've left
no note until he's fucking dead

The Hole

they've put Jeremy Wren in a box
   the children ask, is Jeremy in the box
      yes, Jeremy's in the box
say the pale adults who hold their leaky faces
above the children's heads   it's hard for Jackself to hold
in his head the box that holds Jeremy Wren

   his shirt collar frets
      his black shoes are Frankenstein to walk in
         Jeremy Wren's
choked his way into a box   he just isn't here
     and who's to say he's in the box   he isn't in the box,
the adults say to the older ones   he's leapt clear
and left his empty body in the box
for us to get rid of   he was always leaving
us to tidy up   but there's a hole in the grass
to hurry his mess into

   is this what they mean by grieving
     wet-combed hair, flannelled ears
and a look at the hole in England where Jeremy Wren will sleep
   will not sleep, but rest   will not rest, but lie
wide awake, staring at the underside of the lid

Jack O'Lantern

the leaves are slimy yellow light
   the year's a sticky door
the wind bangs in the barest trees
   and shakes the apple core

        no   again   the leaves are slime
   the year a bloodshot eye
the trees the rooms of bedlamites
   with bars across the sky

the wind's inside the apple core
   the moon bangs like a drum
and   no   again   the sky's a door
   the year a slum

the wind a house of bedlamites
   with trees in every room
the leaves attached like leather straps
   and light a yellow spoon

the moon's beside the   no   again
   the year breaks down the door
the leaves are shut inside the trees
   the trees in apple cores

the wind bangs in the barest rooms
    of bedlam   no   again
the leaves are rooms, the   no   the moon's
    a   no   the year a vein

of narrow gold, the trees gold flakes
    the leaves gold leaves, the wind
a whiny   no   again   the rakes
    are brooms, the moon is skinned

and   no again   the bedlamites
    have wedged the no   again
the wind is bare and yellow spoons
    are banging on the brain

the year's wedged shut with apple cores
    the no a leather stain
the slimy moon an open sore
    and every room the same

Redbreast

Jackself's in the outdoors, mucky snow
still hanging on sticks and slushed
against the roadside,
the wind in his face, his hands claws
and there's nowhere to go that isn't toe-

stubbing stone
or a dripping blackwood   the fields stuck
full of stalks,
the sky torn polythene, flapping   how long
since Jeremy Wren went into the earth

like a seed potato   no   like a sunflower seed   no
like a seed potato   livid-skinned, with unseeing eyes
and hair-sprouts   Jackself has three lines of a song
that aren't even three
because one's a repeat
   sing them anyhow, Jackself

     I see a robin redbreast in a blackthorn tree
       I see a robin redbreast in a blackthorn tree
         the seasons turn but all year round it's wintertime in me

The Misery

Jackself has rent his jeans, is shrunk
into an armchair in Lamanby while the year wheels
round and the days pass like light
between the spokes   ash under his eyes
and his fingernails, sweepings for his meals,
his face battered, sorrow-bright

   he needs a quest, thinks Jeremy Wren,
who's been watching Jackself from the coals
of the stove

   across the fields, into a copse where a black pond lies
staring, Wren drifts with the chimney smoke
and settles like goose-down on the water   wake
up, Wren says, and the pond
blinks

   to the door of Lamanby they come, tales
of chewed off tractor tyres, blood clots
in the milk, trampled corn, midnight snuffles
at virgins' bedroom windows, weird
fires in unpeopled places, slime
on doorbells and apple trees, headaches,
power cuts, bankruptcies, skid marks
on the seesaw and whipworms in the ale

squeaky voices from the topside of the world
tell them, but Jackself lifts his grief-mask
a little to listen   he's at the keyhole
for Jenny Reid's testimony at the kitchen table

    she glimpsed the monster
                    goat's ears,
                    chapped lips
by the mothy glow of the village phone box

    there's a tickle   electric, thawing
and Jackself's deep blue
indifference to brushing his teeth and wearing clean socks
is dislodged in a slump like a snow crust

    from his weapon chest,
the sheath knife, Eglantine   from his wardrobe,
his denim jacket, torch, tool belt, tin camping cup,
rucksack, horned hat and Gore-Tex breastplate

    for six days and nights he tracks the fiend,
dipping his cup at cattle troughs, gnawing
the kernels from beech nuts, the marrow
from earthworms, and at dusk
on the seventh day he enters the copse

       fishhook twigs, deveining briars
                    cold fuming from the leaf-mulch floor,
then the knockerless basalt door
of the pond on which he hammers
twice with the bone hilt of Eglantine

       tarry bubbles
break

and from them, word by word, a voice like a fart
asks   who is this halfwit who brings his heart
happy to my larder

       hey, Jackself cries,
I bet you lick the undersides
of stones, the black chassis of trucks in laybys,
asking who am I

       deep in the pond, past shelf
after grisly shelf, the monster is laired,
listening
       how does he know,
it thinks

    hey, Jackself cries,
I bet you're loved like a motorway
service station litterbin

    yes, the monster says to itself,
whoever you are, you understand

    hey, Jackself cries, I bet you sing
with the wind through the rust-holes
in the corrugated iron roof
of a shed where no one goes

    I do,
the monster says
    I do

                        but that won't stop me
skinning you

    and up, up
into the lightening
green silence kicks
the creature, dismembering hands
clasped like a bride's

and Jackself is thrown back
at its bursting through,
the pond smashed miles
into the night and falling
as foul rain onto his face,
and his body mounted and churned
deeper into the slurry by the Misery's
writhing down on top of him
with all its gristly weight

    but skin me, Jackself says,
and you'd see I'm
monster underneath

    and he rips out the Misery's
throat with his teeth

Jackself's Boast

I am hero, a harrower of hellish meres
and dragon haunts,
demolisher of demons, overlord
of ogres, wyverns   I feel sick
moans Jackself as he stumbles home
in the dark, the Misery's head heavy in his rucksack

    sawing it off
he'd blunted his knife on the spinal cord
then fouled his jeans and lost his footing
in slicks of blood as he'd hauled
at the flaps of hacked-open hide,
his knife-hand so slippery he'd nicked
the bowel and gagged at the reek
that hosed out, steaming

    hard to feel heroic
when you're up to your armpits
in dog meat, and what's Jackself
to show for it but a suit of gore
that's stiffened to him,
a ratty, still wet skin
and between his shoulder blades
the weight of the dead
face he's sure is Jeremy Wren's

no
            if it was his, he'd be calling
Jackself softshite
and worse through the webbing   but Wren is gone
and here Jackself is slammed
by his loss as he hasn't been
and starts bawling
into his crusty, stinking hands

   by the time he's under the outside light
of Lamanby, Jackself's shaken his heart
clean and full of fresh night air,
and on the doorstep
he undoes his rucksack to find
a rabbit's head

A Haunting

Jackself is sitting on the wall
outside Lamanby, watching the thingamybob, whatsit-
called, rising

    it's prettier than a suicide's face,
Jeremy Wren says, but there's something about it
of the death's head   shut up,
Jackself says, you're *still*
full of shit
    me, Wren says   you're the one moping

    you shouldn't even be here, should you,
Jackself says   aren't there rules

    this is a haunting,
Wren says, and it's perfectly within the law,
such as it is   with his forefinger Wren is stroking a great
moth that purrs
like a cat   have you, Jackself says quietly, met anyone

    do you think I'd be here gassing to you if Marilyn Monroe was upstairs
        Jesus, it's like   well, never mind

           like what, Jackself says
    just watch the pretty stone
and forget it, Wren says

they sit,
gazing up at the unmentionable
    when I'm on the toilet, Jackself says, I imagine you
watching me

    yes, Wren says, we all are   me, Shakespeare,
Einstein, Joan of Arc   we all make sure to never miss
a poo

    I think it's giving me
issues,
Jackself says   don't talk to me about issues, Wren says,
look at this old sheet I have to wear

    it's then the moth
wobbles into the dark air
and up towards the unutterable thing
    you know I've got nothing
on under it, Wren shouts,
as Jackself slams Lamanby's front door behind him

Spring-heeled Jack

above Jackself, the night's
night all the way to the moon
and stars   he's on tiptoes,
scrabbling a crater-rim
for finger-holds
   if I can just climb
into her face,
I won't have to suffer
her one sad stare

   Wren's at the ghost-hole
watching Jackself as he dangles
by his fingertips, kicks his feet,
then lets go
and drops   oof   to the stubble, claps
the dust off his hands, then leaps
again for the uppermost
edge of the moon   but the sky's begun
to float it further and further
away from him
into the blue

    I wish you weren't a ghost

     I know you do

[55]

The Desk

Jeremy Wren sings
under his breath

    gone gone
the sabretooth
and gone
the mastodon

    you don't have any breath,
Jackself says

    it's a figure of speech,
Wren says

    Jackself, have you something
to say to the class

    no Miss

        then put your hands on your desk
where we can see them

       inscribed
with pen-knifed knot-work,
its underside fabulous
to the touch with carbuncles
of gum, his desk is where
Jackself keeps what
Wren has bequeathed him

       I didn't bequeath you anything,
Wren says   my rubber, my calculator, my shatterproof
ruler and my spider
in a matchbox   you just took them

       what were you going to do,
Jackself murmurs, spend your death
catching up on your maths homework

       it's not long enough,
Wren says, and Jackself snorts

       JACKSELF!

              it's Jeremy, he says, and the class goes stiff
with fear   they all think you're going to cry
and embarrass them, Wren says   do it
and I'll let you keep my stuff

Jack Snipe

Jackself tramps down
to the water's edge
in time to watch the day go
out of the estuary

   a goose honks
from way up
in the night that laps
at his feet and he drops

after it a pebble
he's brought from the mainland
of sunlight, then heels off
his trainers, balls up his socks,
rolls up his jeans and wades
in among the stars oh
                 oh

                    how cold the heavens are
and squidgy between his toes

Skipjack

the fish owe Jackself
   he wants gills,
another element
for a home, the sea
to hold him for a good long while

   these demands he takes to the rocky shore
at low tide, where the pools gaze
with new lenses at their grotto walls
flinching with jellies

   Jackself rives a limpet
from a crevice in the shell-inlaid floor
   the sole of its yellow foot
is a callus that flexes
and draws in
as he cranks his rusty blade around the socket

   what comes out is neither eye
nor tongue, but has salt tears
and a root

   Jackself chews and swallows it,
then drinks a palmful of sea
from a trap of stone

in the distance the great gears
full of cockleshells turn
and the pool at his feet begins to churn

and swell, then swivels round
to look at him, and roaring in his ears
a voice from fathoms down

speaks coelacanth and dead zone
and conger in a cannon mouth

and in no time the tide is in
and lifting into the dark
brown blistered ropes of bladderwrack
and tiny velvet crabs

but guess who's nearly halfway home,
the big noise at his back

The Comeback Deal

it's not as if this is a Jesus-type
comeback deal   Wren is not Jesus

   have you thought of a new name yet,
Jackself asks   I think Jesus
has a good ring to it, Wren says, Jesus Aballava

   Jackself doesn't laugh
      this is not a resurrection situation,
and we have to stop saying Jesus, he says

   Jesus, don't get your sackcloth
in a twist, Wren says

   you know you can't just walk in
to the life you had, Jackself says   cats will hiss,
light-bulbs flicker,
your mum get a feeling of impending doom
every time she picks your dirty pants and socks up off your bedroom floor

   which would be loads
of times, Wren says, and squints
at the fields stricken
with crispiness and cold smoke

Tithe

hullo

Jackself says   cocks his head

                    nothing

                              without

doors

slammed curtains

soot-fall certain

silence

                    his

smooth end

searches his

middle room   nope

                                                        ear-pop

of absence

            how

                    this morning

                            tripped

the kettle

without   giving

                                                        nothing

        months

dead now   his due

Jack O'Bedlam

Jackself is squabbling in the rookery
he's bald and black and stroppy
    the wind was wound
    six times around
before he hatched his copy

Now I can make him do my naughty
his eyes will not betray me
    they're just like mine
    but minus nine
times twelve to the power of maybe

Who dropped that eyelash in the basement
who thought that thought behind the door
    with phantom ears
    poor Jackself hears
the dandelions roar

He's up in the lofts of Lamanby
rifling through the sun
    I pick my way
    from day to day
undoing what's been done

For heart, Jackself has a hairy nettle
his face is greener stuff
    a long time goes
    between his toes
but never feels enough

Sow the darkness, grow a stone
Jackself is fishing for worms
    he baits his hook
    with a dirty look
and lowers it into the germs

Tell a story, Doublejack
until our sofas burst
    the words are cold
    but get it told
or it will tell you first

Bind these days in the book of moons
poor Jackself needs to sleep
    if north is south
    then Jackself's mouth
is fifty forests deep

Line a coat, unlace a shoe
Jackself, take off your belt
    your mighty skin
    is mighty thin
when your studs and buckles melt

I'm in the house of Bethlehem
lying in a manger
    it's my turn then
    to turn again
and meet myself a stranger

Jackself, please write an inventory
of all your moving parts
    there's only one
    and it's not my tongue
but my stillness never starts

Just like the rain on holidays
it's guaranteed to fall
    Jackself decides
    to stay inside
which is really no choice at all

Wren is hopping on the window ledge
come out, come out, he cries
    poor Jackself swears
    there's no one there
and fills in both his eyes

Underneath my keyhole suit
I'm nothing but a knock
    if I go through
    will you come too
and snap off the key in the lock

Jackself is dancing down the lonning
at the bottom of the world
    the day is dust
    and Jackself must
be back before he's old